YOUR KNOWLEDGE HAS VALUE

Bibliographic information published by the German National Library:

The German National Library lists this publication in the National Bibliography; detailed bibliographic data are available on the Internet at http://dnb.dnb.de .

Imprint:

Copyright © 1990 GRIN Verlag
Print and binding: Books on Demand GmbH, Norderstedt Germany
ISBN: 9783346043405

This book at GRIN:

https://www.grin.com/document/501416

Volker Beckmann

Forms of humour in Sinclair Lewis' novels "Main Street" and "Babbitt"

GRIN Verlag

GRIN - Your knowledge has value

Since its foundation in 1998, GRIN has specialized in publishing academic texts by students, college teachers and other academics as e-book and printed book. The website www.grin.com is an ideal platform for presenting term papers, final papers, scientific essays, dissertations and specialist books.

Visit us on the internet:

http://www.grin.com/

http://www.facebook.com/grincom

http://www.twitter.com/grin_com

Universität Bielefeld

Fakultät für Linguistik
und Literaturwissenschaft

**An Essay on some Forms of Humor in Sinclair Lewis` "Main Street"
and "Babbitt"**

Volker Beckmann

Table of Contents

Introduction

Austin tentatively suggests in an essay entitled "Sinclair Lewis and Western Humor" that the novelist "was a humorist first and a satirist only secondarily".[1] The scholar confirms his view by pointing to the fact that the relationship between Carol and Will in <u>Main Street</u> and between father and son in <u>Babbitt</u> end in a conciliatory spirit and that the happy ending is a "convention in a comic novel".[2]

Before we continue our discussion about whether Lewis could be considered primarily a humorist or a satirist, let us first consult Shipley`s <u>Dictionary of World Literary Terms</u> which provides a general definition of the term "<u>humor</u>":

> First applied to the subject of laughter in the 18th century to distinguish the genial and affirmative forms of comic writing, then greatly in vogue, from satire, mockery and ridicule. Now widely used as a generic term for everything that appeals to man`s disposition toward comic laughter. The change testifies to an increasing recognition, due largely to the influence of psychology and particularly the scientific observation of infants, that laughter is, in its simple biological form, genial and affirmative.[3]

However, we have already found out, that Lewis uses a certain form of <u>irony</u> in his opening passages of <u>Main Street</u> where the old clichés of "pioneering", "lassies in sunbonnets", and "bears killed with axes" are replaced by the new cliché of the "rebellious girl" who epitomizes the spirit of the Middlewest.

Now "irony ... can extend in theory from pure compassion to pure denunciation, but in practice contains some measure, however slight, of both."[4] "Irony is not at all of one piece, but can register varying degrees of distance or severity, ranging from a satirical bitterness to a benevolent awareness of contradictory impulses..."[5]

Also three definitions of <u>irony</u> given in <u>Collins Dictionary of the English Language</u> may be taken into account.[6]

- "the humorous or mildly sarcastic use of words to imply the opposite of what they normally mean." e.g. "Main Street is the climax of civilization." (Main Street, prologue)
- "an instance of this, used to draw attention to some incongruity or irrationality." e.g. "The car was insultingly cheerful on the drive." (Babbitt, ch. 7, 3)

- "incongruity between what is expected to be and what actually is, or a situation showing such incongruity." e.g. "Ezra Stowbody was a troglodyte." (Main Street, ch. 4, 4) or "Mrs. Bogart was not the acid type of Good Influence." (Main Street, ch. 6, 71)

The authorial tone which is "the stance or attitude taken by an (implied) author towards his reader, and towards (parts of) his message"[7] might be characterized as humorously detached, incongruent, and ironic as far as the prologue to Main Street is concerned. The distance between the (implied) author and his message is also increased because the prologue is "a gem of satiric exaggeration".[8]

The term satire originated from Latin Cookery Language, perhaps from the collocation "lanx satura, a full dish, a platter of mixed fruits as an offering to a rural god."[9] Thus the basic sense of the term satire is that of medley or mixture.

In the prologue to Main Street a car occurs together with a general and a humanist; also it is strange and incongruous that the word of a village grocer is said to be respected in places as far away as London and Prague.

To sum up then, we might say that the authorial tone characteristic of Lewis' fiction is one showing an attitude of detachment which is achieved by the (implied) author with the help of satire, irony, or exaggeration reflecting a wide spectrum of tone ranging from bitter denunciation to more genial, benevolent forms of humor, or to an awareness of incongruous, contradictory impulses.

The implied reader, on the other hand, is expected to appreciate the stylistic values of authorial tone, distance and point of view.

In the following passages I would like to see what kind of satirical methods Lewis makes use of and show some examples taken from Main Street and Babbitt which reflect such forms of humor as satirical bitterness, ironical incongruity, and joking, playful language.

Notes to introduction

1. Austin, J.C.: Sinclair Lewis and Western Humor, in: Madden, D.: American Dreams, American Nightmares. Carbondale and Edwardsville 1970, p. 104.
2. ibid., p. 104.
3. Shipley, J.T. (ed.): Dictionary of World Literary Terms. Forms. Technique. Criticism. Boston 1970, pp. 150-151.
4. Leech, G. N.; Short, M. S.: Style in Fiction. London and New York (Longman) 1985, 4th impression, p. 283.
5. ibid., p. 283.
6. Dictionary of the English Language (Collins) 1979, pp. 771-772.
7. Leech; Short, op. cit., p. 280.
8. Austin, loc. Cit., p. 102.
9. Shipley (ed.), op. cit., p. 286.

1. Contrast as a satirical device

The novel <u>Main Street</u>, or at least the first 19 chapters of it, is regarded as a "devastating satire on the small town"[1] and a 'satirical problem novel'[2] by literary critics. Also two scholars seem to agree on the evaluation that <u>Main Street</u> cannot be labelled realistic fiction.[3]

Satire as a generic term is defined by Collins Dictionary of the English Language as

> a novel, play, entertainment, etc., in which topical issues, folly, or evil are held up to scorn by means of ridicule and irony. (p. 1297)

Yoshida writes that Lewis

> As a natural satirist … he exaggerates the follies of the townspeople, contrasts their shortcomings with the desirable strong points necessary for them to live up to the ideal standard cherished in the author's mind, and as a result the person he portrays turns into a caricature.[4]

Correspondingly, the dreams of the protagonist, Carol, are so contrasted with the mentality and behaviour of the village population that she experiences disillusionment more than once. Dooley describes Carol as being 'impulsive, undiplomatic, and ignorant of complications'[5] , Schorer characterizes her as being 'naïve', if not 'downright silly'.[6]

When Carol tries to persuade the town millionaire Dawson to finance an ambitious building scheme, she learns that he flatly refuses to encourage her vague town improvement projects. Dawson's answer shows that he is content with the status quo.

> Why now, child, you've got a lot of notions. Besides, what's the matter with the town? Looks good to me. I've had people that have travelled all over the world tell me time and again that Gopher Prairie is the prettiest place in the Middlewest.[7]

Dooley labels Carol 'a caricature of a reformer, a take-off on the advanced young woman'.[8]

However naïve and young Carol may be, kindness and responsibility are her most pleasing traits because she looks after the Bjornstam family more lovingly and tenderly than any other representative of one of the local denominations.

Also, Carol is portrayed in such a lively and sympathetic way by Lewis that we as readers can only fully believe the statement made by Lewis' wife Grace Hegger Lewis who confided that her husband 'thought Carol's Chinese party a very fine party indeed and one he would have enjoyed attending.'[9]

At the party Carol is trying hard to divert her guests as best she can by introducing new forms of entertainment in order to prevent the mechanical performance of rigid stunts.

> Now we're going to play an idiotic game which I learned in Chicago. You will have to take off your shoes, for a starter! After that you'll probably break your knees and shoulder-blades.[10]

Later Will reveals to Carol that her guests laughed about her being dressed up as the Chinese Princess Poo and, as a result, Carol resents their poking fun at her. When the play that she directs and stages in Gopher Prairie fails to meet the expectations of the audience including Miles Bjornstam, her dream of improving the cultural affairs of the town are shattered once again. As a member of the town library-board Carol tries in vain to persuade the other members to contribute $ 15 each for the purchase of new books.

Whereas Yoshida describes Carol as "an archetype of a woman who tries to revolt against the archetype of the town and the people"[11], Schorer labels the central characters in Main Street "familiar American types – the complacent husband of common sense and the discontented wife with romantic dreams."[12]

Yoshida explains that apart from the device of contrast Lewis makes use of the methods of invective, caricature, parody, and mimicry.

2. Invective

According to Yoshida, Lewis passes his satirical message on to the reader by making use of types or caricatures, but sometimes the narrator himself ridicules "unfavorable aspects of the town, its institutions, education, churches, religion, banks, rotary club, homes, customs and manners."[13]

Webster defines the term invective as 'a vehement and bitter denunciation or attack, which is often public, and may be in good cause and expressed in refined language'.[14]

In a well-known passage (Main Street, ch. 22, III, pp. 257-258), which we might consider now, the satire attacks the standardized materialism, provincialism, boring provincial rigidity, and the narrow-mindedness of the people. The satirical message, which is admittedly quite acid and vitriolic, is emphasized by the adjectives "savorless", "tasteless", "coatless", "thoughtless", and "mechanical".

3. Caricature

Webster gives the following definition of caricature, 'a picture or other figure or description in which the peculiarities of a person or thing are so exaggerated as to appear grotesque or ridiculous'.[15] Yoshida explains that "a type is a product of exaggeration, and exaggeration is a method of satire. In addition a type victimized by satire becomes a ruthless description of a helpless caricature".[16]

The best example of a caricature is of course Babbitt who, according to Dooley, is "portrayed as an archetype of the Booster", the average businessman, "loudmouthed, unthinking, insensitive".[17] His speech reflects the prejudices and clichés of his social group. Although Babbitt tries to revolt against conformity, he is finally persuaded by his friends of the Athletic Club to join the Good Citizen League.

Babbitt, the real-estate dealer, appreciates his car because it is more than of functional value to him or because it is a status symbol; he seems to be deeply emotionally attached to his car, "…, his motor car was poetry and tragedy, love and heroism" to him. (chapter 3, pp. 1-2 <Penguin Modern Classics> Harmondsworth 1987)

When he is feeling sick, everything appears to be dull, boring and "mechanical" to him. (cf. ch. 18, p. 180)

At the beginning of chapter 29 Babbitt is portrayed in such a way that it becomes clear to the reader that the protagonist is playing with the idea of leaving the solid, well paved road of bourgeois success. He has caught himself a mistress and is speaking well of a lawyer who represents labour interests. But at the end of chapter 33 Babbitt has slipped back into role of the average businessman who denounces labour unions, is hostile to immigration, and loves golf and money.

4. Parody

Lewis also makes extensive use of parody in his novels. Here parody cannot be defined as

> Composition in prose or verse in which the characteristic turns of thought and phrase in an author or class of authors is imitated in such a way as to make them appear ridiculous, especially by applying them to ludicrously inappropriate subjects (OED)[18]

In Lewis' fiction parody is used when compositions of prose, excerpts taken from newspaper articles summarize social events, such as parties or dramatic performances, in an over-polite and euphemistic way. For example, "The Gopher Prairie Dauntless" provides an over-polite appreciation rather than a severe critique of the play "The girl from Kankakee". Although Carol admits that the dramatic performance is a failure, the newspaper article praises it with smooth hackneyed phrases such as "vision of loveliness", "pretty as a picture", "suited in the role". The article also includes familiar abbreviations, namely "doc" and the word "tootsie" representing baby talk. (Main Street, ch. 18, IV, pp. 222-223)

5. Mimicry

Mimicry, too, is an integral part of Lewis' fiction. Collins English Dictionary defines the term as "the act or art of copying or imitating closely". (p. 937) Especially oratory or elocution is given satirical treatment in Lewis' novels.

Babbitt who helps the local Republican candidate for mayor to win the local elections is touring the city of Zenith in the election campaign delivering speeches to the public. In one of his speeches he characterizes his view of "Our Ideal Citizen". (cf. ch. 14, III, p. 142) There he portrays a rather easy-going, sporty family man, who is also a good business man, likes reading newspapers and lowbrow Western novels, and loves taking his family to the movies every now and then. In his speech Babbitt uses a lot of informal words, such as "sassiety teas", "zip", "kiddies", "sneaks in", "mite" and even a slang word, namely "cuss". Lewis intends to satirize "the materialistic desires, triteness and the easy-going way of life of the people."[19]

Another fine example of <u>mimicry</u> can be found in <u>Babbitt</u> in chapter 30, subchapter 4, where a Mrs. Mudge invited by a "League of the Higher Illumination" is giving a speech on "the matter of Spiritual Saturation". Clearly enough, esoteric language is satirized there.

According to Yoshida baby talk that is used by lovers, husband and wife or between very friendly persons in Lewis' novels also falls into the category of <u>mimicry</u>.

In chapter 9, 2 in <u>Main Street</u> Carol is eavesdropping on the boys Earl Haddock and Cy and is quite surprised to learn that her husband used to chew and spit before they got married.

We might consider another example of baby language occurring in <u>Babbitt</u>, ch. 18, 5.

6. Banter, Slang, Colloquialism

According to Yoshida, colloquial speech is the life and soul of Lewis' literature. In <u>Babbitt</u> the reader finds a fine example of banter on page 50, where Babbitt and Paul exchange playful, joking language.

'How's the old horse-thief?'

'All right, I guess. How're you, you poor shrimp?'

'I'm first-rate, you second-hand hunk o'cheese.'

"Reassured thus of their high fondness, Babbitt grunted, 'You're a fine guy, you are! Ten minutes late!" „Riesling snapped, ‚Well, you're lucky to have a chance to lunch with a gentleman!'"

7. "Homely Metaphor"

Rourke classifies Lewis as a writer who belongs to the American fabulists, "particularly those of the frontier".[20] Rourke shows that Lewis uses "homely metaphors". The novelist describes 'an old farmer, solid, wholesome, but not clean – his face like a potato fresh from the earth.'[21]

Now I have reached the end of my short essay and hope that we have gained a first impression of some aspects of Mr. Sinclair Lewis' artistic humor.

Notes

1. Dooley, D.J.: The Art of Sinclair Lewis. Lincoln (The University of Nebraska Press) 1967, p. 60.
2. ibid., p. 70.
3. ibid., p. 70; cf. Yoshida, H.: A Sinclair Lewis Lexicon with a Critical Study of his Style and Method. Tokyo: Hoyn 1976, pp. 12-13.
4. Yoshida, p. 40.
5. Dooley, p. 63.
6. Schorer, M. in an Afterword of the Signet Classic Edition of Main Street. New York 1980, p. 439.
7. Lewis, S.: Main Street. New York 1980, p. 139.
8. Dooley, p. 63.
9. ibid., p. 64.
10. Lewls, p. 78.
11. Yoshida, p. 13.
12. Schorer, p. 439.
13. Yoshida, p. 13.
14. ibid., p. 13.
15. ibid., p. 17.
16. ibid., p. 18.
17. Dooley, p. 83.
18. cited in:Yoshida, p. 24.
19. ibid., p. 31.
20. Rourke, C.: American Humor. New York (Harcourt & Brace) 1931, p. 284.
21. ibid., p. 285.